RADIATION KING

Also by JASON GRAY

Photographing Eden
How to Paint the Savior Dead
Adam & Eve Go to the Zoo

For my nephew Henry,
who hadn't quite joined us yet
when the last one came out

&

In Memoriam
Karen (Bald) Mapes,
English teacher extraordinaire,
who left us too soon

ACKNOWLEDGMENTS

My grateful thanks to the editors of the following journals for first publishing some of these poems:

American Journal of Poetry: "Able Archers" & "US Radium's Finest Personnel Man to the New Recruits"

Birmingham Poetry Review: "Cold Fusion"

Botticelli: "You have to start," "A sunbather takes," "To stay even-keeled," "The sun: An umbrella—" & "Shells are filling up"

Hoot: "The little flames"

Jet Fuel Review: "Yellow" & "Blue"

Kenyon Review: "The Visible Spectra"

Literary Matters: "The Pillars of Creation"

New Criterion: "Relativity"

Sonora Review: "Letters to the Fire IV"

Some of the *Atoms* poems appeared on the Tupelo Press 30/30 blog during February 2015. Thank you to Kirsten Miles, Marie Gauthier, and my fellow 30/30s for welcoming me into that fold.

Some of these poems had their beginnings at the Sewanee Writers' Conference and some had their endings at the Vermont Studio Center. Thank you to those fine institutions.

My deepest gratitude to Piotr Florczyk for selecting this book as the winner of the Idaho Prize for Poetry, and to Christine Holbert & Lost Horse Press for bringing it to life.

My love to the people who made this work, and life, better during the long time of this book's drafting: Doug Basford, Kathy Fagan, Andrew Hudgins, Heather Price, Natalie Shapero, Ida Stewart, Jen Town, and Juliet Williams. Thanks to Maggie Smith for her editorial insight. And especially JL Conrad and Cynthia Marie Hoffman for their poems and for PGMAC. And most of all, to Shannon Reavis, my brother, Tim, and my parents, Bob and Barbara Gray.

Cover Art: Land of the Rising Radiation, digital art by John Ayo.
Author Photo: Cynthia Marie Hoffman.
Book Design: Christine Holbert.

FIRST EDITION

This and other fine Lost Horse Press titles may be viewed online at www.losthorsepress.org.

LIBRARY OF CONGRESS CATALOGING-IN-PUBLICATION DATA may be obtained from the Library of Congress.

ISBN: 978-0-9991994-3-5

TABLE OF CONTENTS

RADIATION KING, or *Tales from the Multiverse*

COLOR IS AN EVENT

ATOMS

LETTERS TO THE FIRE

AN ALTERNATE ENDING

To begin with, you must realize that atom splitting is just another way of causing an explosion. While an atom bomb holds more death and destruction than man has ever before wrapped in a single package, its total power is definitely limited. Not even hydrogen bombs could blow the earth apart or kill us all by mysterious radiation.

—*Survival Under Atomic Attack,*
Civil Defense Office, *NSRB Doc. 130*

If it's not love, then it's the bomb that will bring us together.

—The Smiths

RADIATION KING,
OR TALES FROM THE MULTIVERSE

PROJECT FAULTLESS

What hurt
to set
a little fire here?

Hot Creek Valley
was Mars
to most of the world.

This was
a test
to see if the ground could hold

A little bomb
in its belly
before we gave it

A greater tonnage
to bear.
The ground could not.

Faults opened,
and the steel
bomb-tube sunk flush

With the dirt
stovepiped
nine feet above the earth.

This was
the land-
scape we imagined when we

Imagined the world
post-
        apocalypse:

Barren, cracked,
a shell
        that magma would

In time
subsume.
        Atoms really are

Perfection:
tiny
        movers, brilliant gods,

Or force
of evolution,
        if you prefer.

We dreamed the science,
pulled apart
        the facts,

Made the future
a fiction
        we'd never live.

Can you blame us
for our triumphs?
        Soon enough

We'll be
irradiated
        ghosts

Hiding
in abandoned
                    silver mines

        Or narrating
from the bunkers.
                We wanted

        To be generous.
We moved the tests
                back south.

        A casino shakes
and maybe a sucker
                gets lucky

        If the wheel jumps
a little,
                to 35,

        To 26,
black, then red,
                stack, unstack.

        Then a crashing
of chips
                the dealer sweeps away.

RELATIVITY

He took the watch apart. The snowflake gears,
Too delicate for hands his size, bend and
Entangle on the table. If only the metal
Would melt then maybe so would time.

The leather band has faded to a pale urine.
The watch had been his father's,
Worn at the Bulge. The gears malfunctioned
When he hurled the watch to slow

Time down—it only stopped. There are just
So many revolutions. Telomeres clip
And age us, but death is not a rabbit
Pulled from your coat on a crowded subway.

RADIOACTIVE SHADOW

San Onofre Nuclear Generating Station

The twin duomos rose along the ocean Dad went to work at
SONGS The pellets of uranium kept cool by sea, bombed by
neutrons This was my inheritance The generous split, like Jesus's
loaves It fed us, clothed us, sheltered us under the brightness of
its shadow

The lights came on each night, each night I prayed to wake before
I died Prayed the concrete hold intact its universe of broken atoms
As this is earth, the beautiful explodes and explodes Each arc of
light an almost flood of dust Blessed enough to be so cursed

CLOUD

We kept our many things in the sky
To resurrect when we needed them.
Invisible but omnipresent beam
Of particles. We lived on the memory
Of waves. The ocean stayed with us to dream.
The day was hot and you burned. Your childhood
Peeled off in the night and became the dust that filled
A coughed-out prayer: great clouds of someone's whim.

Looking up from the ship deck there were reefs
In the air, palm trees, whole islands, now we were
The best makers of clouds in all the world.
The girls on the beach wear Bikini debris.
Once we worried we would be vaporized.
Thank God we can now be digitized.

Thank God we can now be digitized.
Fit on a drive we call a thumb. Blesséd
Metonymy, a way to shelter in place
Forever, until—our hopes entrusted
To climate control—an EMP thieves the sweet
Air-conditioned databank dream from us.

How late the world is coming to itself.
The way a wave after breaking glides non-
Chalantly up the shore. You searched in vain
For an intact shell to place on your souvenir shelf
And then were swept from the seaside when the horizon
Showed cumulonimbus calvus on its line.
Last summer you made yourself memorize
The shapes, all the many shapes of the sky.

PRUSSIAN BLUE

The doctors give us dust
                    masks now that the world
Is an exploded mine.
                    We take the pills and flush
Our blood with the color
                    of the Virgin Mary.
Our bruised knees could not
                    provide such intercession.
The fine art
                    of chemistry consumed
The heaviness within
                    and made our bowels shit blue.

It turned midnight and the cold
                    did not frighten us
Enough. The good
                    Christ in his tomb
Are those in the fallout
                    shelters and the airlock
Hatch spun and opened
                    and no one was gone.
We lucky few remaining
                    take our turn

At the wheel.
                    We have forestalled the hour
Of our death but
                    we have not been saved.

ABLE ARCHERS

The Forbidding of Distance Weapons, Namely Crossbows and Longbows
—Pope Innocent II, *Canon 29, Second Lateran Council*

Attacking from afar is, if not unholy,
At least unfair. Barbed arrows launched from bows
—Cowgut vibrato harmony behind—
Are not the way to kill a Christian. Face
To face, the sword, the axe, a dagger from
A sleeve. The Vatican knew the way to mass
Murder was through the sky, and so sealed it
To all but the Holy Spirit, birds, and saints
Ascending. Papal bullets never last:

Planning for disaster, ranks of archers
In the rear guard wait for the slightest twitch
Of the sun on metal from the other side—
Or, say, some restless horses stamp their iron-
Clad knights a little forward, like a curtain
Billowing, is that enough to raise the stakes
For a volley? The captain's sword swipes down
Like a second hand. And does it matter
If the missiles come arcing
                                         tipped with fire?

THE PILLARS OF CREATION

The universe is not collapsing back.
From the verandas of the violet
Republic, we are coming to know the end
Already happened years ago, the light
Only now catching up to us.

The pillars meet a supernova
And at light speed seem to die
For a long time. By the time Andromeda
Is our permanent firework, someone
Is watching us, and we are ghosts.

OHIO ST., CHICAGO

Clots of pedestrians are worse
Than traffic lights. We may not make
Your departure time. I like to think
A mouse turns a wheel, but I know better
The clock sits in the shadow
Of an electron if at all. Physics suggests
Everything should run backward
Just as well, but the egg resists
Recombobulation. Time
Is infused in our circulation.

I merged into the wrong lane.
We're late; you'll have to run. I'm left
With a billion seconds (roughly) and they
Are not enough. Not when my heart
Pumps harder as you step
Out of the car: one leg and then
The other and then closing them
Back together like midnight.
One day my heart will stop.

COLD FUSION

No, not the one about *fucking in snow,*
Though that's a good one, but the meld
Of hydrogen, the sun's great orgy,
Here colder, containable—smash
Those atoms and get a squeaky voice.
That's how we'll greet the aliens,
In the future when the only energy
Crisis left will be in the bedroom,
And the Little Grays' report back
Will read, *Their massive bodies belied*
The tiny tongues. For with limitless fuel,
Why not ingest a little more?
I'm jealous for your proton: green
And made of us. And that same sun
Which shines a rainbow on leaked oil
Tomorrow will say cheap goods
Or children *fucking ends now.*

US RADIUM'S FINEST PERSONNEL MAN
TO THE NEW RECRUITS

US Radium needs you girls for good-
Pay factory work. This is the future, girls,
The Age of Radiation! You'll make

All of America's wristwatch dials glow
With Undark, this company's trademark paint,
Created from a brand new element.

A lady like yourselves discovered it
Over in France, now isn't that something?
They gave her the Nobel Prize, honest to God.

It isn't dangerous, give it a taste.
A lick of the brush won't hurt you, and it'll make
A finer point. Try a little dab

On your nails, perhaps your teeth, too, to entice
A young man in the dark of the picture show.
Delights he didn't even know were there!

Those aprons all the men are wearing?
That's just to keep the paint off their clothes
When they mix it up in the warehouse.

We men are the real vain creatures, aren't we, girls?
Now take your places and get to work.
Smile girls, and glow in the dark for me.

THE VISIBLE SPECTRA

The ajar church door and absolute dark
Interior except the quad-light through
Stained glass. The aisle shapeless
And the altar gone.

The latest math finds ninety-five percent
Of the universe subluminous: dark matter,
Dark energy. We don't know what it is,
Except it isn't dark.

COLOR IS AN EVENT

WHITE

The whitest white is made by grinding bones of unblessed children.
It will keep no light.

The paint is toxic for a thousand years. But that is not the reason
It's called blight.

Our binding agent is a secret. In-house its name is Ghost.
There is no white.

RED

When Adam's blood first ran
From scratching at the walls,
    He called it red,
Color's oldest name.
It would be much used.

Cochineals were killed
To dress the Inquisition
    For a long trip
To Hell, the flames already
Dipped into the cloth.

You should have left ten years
Before your blood went gray.
    The Wolf can see you
Riding Hood, so run
Run run, run Red run.

ORANGE

My children love the taste of orange.
They like it flooding chins, the orange
Juice dripping, sticking, tickling. Orange
To flavor chocolate candy, orange
To scent their mother's hair. The orange
Crayon is just a stub, they orange
Color everything they see orange.
Their teacher stocks special orange
Chalk for them—they concentrate on orange
Problems better, take one orange
Away from a crate and orange
How many do you have? The orange
Walls of their room are orange and orange.
The neighbors call them sunrise orange
And sunset orange. There would be no orange
Living without their love and orange
We do what love requires orange.

YELLOW

The sun is yellow.

> The sun is a blotch

Of paint, the paint

> Is egg yolk and

Orpiment crushed

> With the utmost

Pressure *for ten years*—

> If you can manage—

So much the better

> Said Cennini

And *don't soil*

> *Your mouth with it.*

This is not for cowards.

> The orpiment

Is arsenic

> Sulfide, a rock

Layered impasto

> With the run-off

From a volcano.

> The sun is a volcano.

The sun is a poison.

> The sun is the sun.

GREEN

Money's less green. The hungry children
Papier-mâché some dollar bills
But make them purple.

I hate the pale green of Easter dyes—
It never richens no
Matter how long you leave the egg.

I was soaked, and could not rise
From my station, left with
Lees in the barrel of wine.

BLUE

Lapis you've covered your lap in matches your eyes,
The skirt you're wearing, lifted over thighs:
Blue lace receding from a white sand beach,
Oh sweet shipwreck. I would de-blue you stitch
By stitch, raise the bluest flame from your skin
With every kiss, flood and loose every vein
Until all left is your cloud-breaking peak.

With broken boots, with sorry song, desire
Leads to the Afghan mine where blue fire
Is blown with black powder into the world
And polished. Bullets were hurled
Here yesterday, perhaps tomorrow too.
Always, until the mountain crumbles to
The ocean, and the ocean throws it back.

INDIGO

If music's why you're here,
Sing your homemade song:
Indigo indigo Lindygo now.
We will try to sing along.

Your morning wake up call
Is better than coffee, sex.
Indigo indigo Lindygo now.
Every wave reflects

The high blue of your voice—
The sky's briefest shade
Indigo | unlike | Lindygo now.
The ground's longest hold.

As if we made you out of woad
    To heal our wound.
If the wave is only in your head,
    Does it make a sound?

We cannot bring ourselves
To re-collect your scattered toys.
They are your backup band
And we listen to your ghost of blues.

VIOLET

A little massacre, or, a massacre
     Of little things, the slow lurch of sea snails
Made them immensely catchable. Exposed
     To air, a squeeze of blood, made them Phoenician,
        Purple and literate.

Smart emperors sport the local dye,
     And in the backwaters, even the small-time chief
Can pull it off. Waddle in the robes
     Or wallow in the stink (the rankness made
From the run-off of crushed *muricidae*
        Reached up and down the Levantine coast),
        Each must look the part.

A purple baby born, struggles to breathe,
     Allergic to the world (would kill him fairly
Young, but not as young as other first-
     Born sons), and dressed in rags. But this was back
        When violet was the rage.

BLACK

Most welcoming of all. It takes you in / without discrimination.
Be-all, end- / all of the spectrum, past the gamma ray, / the hole
drawn not with charcoal, soot, burnt vine / or bone. This is the
nothing there is to see. / Fall in, and it will look to us like forever.

ATOMS

You have to start
      Somewhere.
A nearly empty ball
That everyone fetches.

A sunbather takes
      The current
And pinks. We keep calling
Space an ocean.

To stay even-keeled,
        A rocket
Over the water adjusts
Its nozzles. The sea

Turns to emeralds.

The sun: An umbrella—
How much
Could it absorb before
A shut down?—blooms.

The wind's clean sweep.

The letters led
     To letters.
But every diamond burned
Into poisonous air

And returned to its sender.

So much of the sky
        Is useless.
A dolphin dives into
The atmosphere

To see the cloudwrecks.

The little flames
        Of foxes
Spied us from the dunes.
I held my breath

In case you needed it.

The wave flashes its white
        Smile
Right before it sweeps
You under. You

Clutch for anything.

Pretty red curls,
    A glowing
Script that writes itself—
Closed—I wait

Still for the slightest
    Flicker.

The streetlights seemed
        To deaden us.
We stripped and threw ourselves
Into the sea

To know if we'd corrode
        Or heal.

Caught in the flash
     Powder
Of the boardwalk photographer—
Blinded, but kept

Forever like a ghost
     Under glass.

Flowers that grow
From gunpowder.
The sky is a hothouse tonight.
One day it may

Be brimstone falling on
Our villas.

Instead of the beach,
          A Slurpee-
Blue hotel pool, so clean
It burns. Our skin

Caramelizing like good,
          Sweet people.

Shells are filling up
    The beach,
But it still looks empty. Air
Hidden in our bones

Like tiny confessional
    Booths.

Shards of antique
      Blue glass
Washed ashore. Collected
To make a mobile

That wards off goblins
           Waiting
Underground for the push
      Of a button.

Broken into.
    The wire
Unreeled like handkerchiefs
From a magician's sleeve.

The charge that travels
    Knot to
Knot like an SOS.

Parisian lace
     And green
With emeralds, a head-
Dress meant for show

Unstitched by a stray
     Retriever
Who hasn't eaten beautiful
     In a week.

The hourglass
        Caressed
And turned. Time passed until
We learned to tell

The time with the quickest
        Blinks. Now
Even whomever we are
Dinosaurs to will know

What time the train
        Arrived
Within a second
        Or two.

The heavy stones
      We try
To skip catch the lip
Of the wave and collapse.

Imagine the rock
      Sinking
Past the fluorescing
Creatures below.

Wishing you were there
          Instead of
      Among the incandescent.

There's only so much
        Of you.
The phonograph needle mined
The groove, revealing

What little we
        Could say
For ourselves. Our satellites
We swaddled in

Gorgeous foil.
        We try
To keep them warm
        At night.

Here is half
        Of me.
Here is another half
For you until

The Earth has ended.
        Let us
Make the largest fire
        From our
                Smallest parts.

LETTERS TO THE FIRE

More than once I've suspected I'm a ghost. Most days
I see no people and even the wind feels like it has gone.
There is nothing close to my face. Is this a beginning or
an end? The coyotes are succeeding, and the crows, and I
suspect the cats are refilling the cities. Lucky to be lost in
the desert I suppose when the world heaved, escaping the pan for the

fire—Haley it would take me two lifetimes
lifetimes to make it around the unimaginable
places to you. And you I must imagine are
dead. I found a map called Indian Country
and relabeled it with truer names. Eight weeks
hiding in Parted Lips, two lifetimes to what I
still call the Heart.

TYPO

||

Now every child raised will be a wolf. Afraid of fire
but able to hunt a shadow off the mountain. Their
senses tripped with a puff of wind. Who knows,
they might be glad to go feral in a radioactive
wonderland. Think the Red Forest in Chernobyl.
The Fukushima kelp beds. Understand I regret
denying you a family, but Haley, the children we might have had would
never have escaped their childhood. Hindsight,
yes, but looking backward stalls the fever I
know is coming. This monocline I need to
navigate I christen the Descendant. I could fall.
I will likely fall.

III

I swear I saw travelers beneath a distant arch. I swear
they moved through and beyond it. All around, the
palette aboriginal ochre and prehistoric shadow. I
followed, imagining a gateway to a world that must
be peopled. There is only rock, and the dust that
rubs away when I touch it. Am I watched? Looking
back, Haley, I worry now it is a fossilized eye of a giant, left to judge us.

A reverse eclipse, rim of shadow around a
blinding light. All the worlds we will never enter
into. I came across a row of airline seats, but
nothing else. Am I called? I keep going, the
Long Stare behind me.

IV

These strange forms—hoodoos—overnight I
dreamt they were remains of people stripped
by furnace-winds streaming from the cities. In
another life I might have called them comical.
Am I the one who disappeared, transported
to a parallel dimension? All the red dust,
the red rock, I am delirious with heat but I
keep walking. I still don't know exactly what
happened and Haley, I turn the cell on each
morning but the radio is silent. Perhaps I never should have left the
riverbank. Even after waiting for the storms
to clear, the air is hot and pricked with dust.
This is the Valley of Medusa, stone-turned
people never getting to go home. I am neither
stone nor getting to go home.

V

At last I've come to a sheltered place. A fast
river and mountains with green décolletage.
Like reaching the bottom of a staircase. It is
not peace, but it may have to do. The days I
climbed down I thought of as the Bread Line.
I became a skeleton, my ribs exposed, yes, but
more my soul had fled to find you. May it
have a swifter journey. And this my dilemma,
Haley, at the top of a trail I saw a city that still had lights. Do I go on,
and if not, would the Bighorn let me stay?
The true anthropocene: we've absconded and
only left a burden. A world littered with our
nursery of fused atoms. The cradle of the new
earth is rocking.

AN ALTERNATE ENDING

NEW PHYSICS

Your body's
Lightness leaning into me is a feather
And a hammer. We are too

Gap-filled. I
Want the physics where I catch neutrinos
That have moved through you. *Oh, my*

Europa,
I want to map the oceans hidden beneath
Your small breasts I loved inside my mouth.

Tilt the hand
That made us full of matter and spin
The haloes of the angels until

The clicking
Stops on 00, the entrance to
The celestial zone that circles this

Alternate
Universe of ours. I want to see
The apple rise into the tree.